Grub to Ladybug

Melvin and Gilda Berger

SCHOLASTIC INC.
New York Toronto London Auckland Sydney
Mexico City New Delhi Hong Kong Buenos Aires

Photographs: Cover: Dwight Kuhn; p. 1: Bios (Etienne)/Peter Arnold, Inc.;
p. 3: Dwight Kuhn; p. 4: D. Bringard/Explorer/Photo Researchers, Inc.; p. 5: Dwight Kuhn;
p. 6: Dwight Kuhn; p. 7: Dwight Kuhn; p. 8: Dwight Kuhn; p. 9: Dwight Kuhn;
p. 10: Dwight Kuhn; p. 11: E.R. Degginger/Dembinsky Photo Assoc.;
p. 12: Dwight Kuhn; p. 13: Dwight Kuhn;
p. 14: Nuridsany ET Perennou/Photo Researchers Inc.;
p. 15: Kim Taylor/Bruce Coleman Inc.; p. 16: Bios (Etienne)/Peter Arnold, Inc.

Photo Research: Sarah Longacre

ISBN 0-439-57487-0

12 11   5 6 7 8 9/0
                                                                                                              08

Printed in the U.S.A.
First printing, March 2004

This ladybug is red
with black spots.

Fun Fact
Ladybugs lay a few eggs at a time.

The mother ladybug
lays eggs on a leaf.

Ladybug eggs are yellow.

The eggs hatch.

Fun Fact

The grub does not look like its mother or father.

A grub comes out of each egg.

Fun Fact

Grubs can eat 60 bugs
in a day.

The grub eats little bugs.

The grub grows bigger.

Fun Fact

Grubs shed their skin
at least three times.

The grub gets a big, new skin.

Then the grub stops growing.

The grub makes a hard shell.
It is called a pupa.

Fun Fact

It takes a few weeks for a pupa to become a ladybug.

The pupa changes into a ladybug.

Fun Fact

Ladybugs are insects.
All insects have
six legs.

The ladybug has six legs.

The ladybug has four wings.

The new ladybug lays eggs on a leaf.